An Essential Guide for the ISFJ Personality Type

Insight into ISFJ Personality Traits and Guidance for Your Career and Relationships

by Sandy Peterson

Table of Contents

Introduction 1

Chapter 1: Understanding the ISFJ Personality Type. 7

Chapter 2: The Strengths and Weaknesses of an ISFJ 11

Chapter 3: The ISFJ as a Friend, Romantic Partner, and Parent 17

Chapter 4: Choosing the Best Career for an ISFJ 23

Chapter 5: The ISFJ's Workplace Behavior and Ethics 27

Conclusion 35

Introduction

The ISFJ personality type can be very intriguing when compared to the other personality types. Here is an individual that does not want to be in the spotlight, yet wants his work to be appreciated and recognized. You have a shy person who is often mislabeled as snobby, and someone who is sensitive to others but has a hard time expressing their own feelings. Truly, the ISFJ seems like a complicated person to anyone who doesn't truly understand where they're coming from.

In truth, the ISFJ individual is no enigma. And although some of their personality traits can seem contradictory, the ISFJ personality type is actually quite easy to decipher. This book will help you uncover the strengths and weaknesses of the ISFJ. Included are detailed descriptions of the ISFJ's unique personality traits that will help you better understand the inner workings of an ISFJ man and woman.

Are you an ISFJ? Or are you in a relationship with an ISFJ? Does he want a long-term relationship with you or not? Does an ISFJ make a good colleague, subordinate, boss, or even a parent? The answers to all these questions and more are what you will find in this book. By the time you're done reading, you will see that the ISFJ personality type is not actually so hard to decode after all. And if you are an ISFJ, understanding the inner workings of your own personality can help you tremendously as you make important decisions, both personally and professionally, as you make your way through life. Save time by cutting down your job searching and just head straight for the careers that are right for your personality type. And save yourself some heartache by learning about how an ISFJ regards love and relationships. If you're ready to gain complete insight into yourself as an ISFJ, or into someone else who is an ISFJ, let's get started!

© Copyright 2015 by Miafn LLC - All rights reserved.

This document is geared towards providing reliable information in regards to the topic and issue covered. The publication is sold with the idea that the publisher is not required to render accounting, officially permitted, or otherwise, qualified services. If advice is necessary, legal or professional, a practiced individual in the profession should be ordered.

- From a Declaration of Principles which was accepted and approved equally by a Committee of the American Bar Association and a Committee of Publishers and Associations.

In no way is it legal to reproduce, duplicate, or transmit any part of this document in either electronic means or in printed format. Recording of this publication is strictly prohibited and any storage of this document is not allowed unless with written permission from the publisher. All rights reserved.

The information provided herein is stated to be truthful and consistent, in that any liability, in terms of inattention or otherwise, by any usage or abuse of any policies, processes, or directions contained within is solely and completely the responsibility of the recipient reader. Under no circumstances will any legal responsibility or blame be held against the publisher for any reparation, damages, or monetary loss due to the information herein, either directly or indirectly.

Respective authors own all copyrights not held by the publisher.

The information herein is offered for informational purposes solely, and is universal as so. The presentation of the information is without contract or any type of guarantee assurance.

The trademarks that are used are without any consent, and the publication of the trademark is without permission or backing by the trademark owner. All trademarks and brands within this book are for clarifying purposes only and are the owned by the owners themselves, not affiliated with this document.

Chapter 1: Understanding the ISFJ Personality Type

The letters ISFJ in Jung's and Briggs Myers' personality type theories stand for Introverted, Sensing, Feeling, and Judging. Based on these words alone, one can infer that the ISFJ is shy, quiet, sensitive, emotional, and perhaps, close-minded. However, the ISFJ need not be strictly defined by these traits. They could also be logical, highly sociable, and acquiescent to new ways of thinking.

The ISFJs are known for their humanity, often showing those around them compassion and generosity. They are always ready to offer assistance, support, and comfort to whoever needs it. It's a blessing then that they make up a large part of the world's population. Individuals that belong to the ISFJ personality type are charitable and they feel fulfillment doing work where they can impart knowledge and kindness. It's not surprising to see these individuals in the fields of academics, social work, and medicine.

One of the most noticeable characteristics of the ISFJs is their tendency to be perfectionists. They are fussy when it comes to details and they will often spend a lot of their time and energy in making sure that all is in order. They often won't settle for satisfactory quality but will instead work to attain the best possible results that they are capable of giving. When it comes to work, the ISFJ person takes it very personally. Perhaps, this is why ISFJs will always submit work that they can be proud of. At home, the ISFJs are not much different. They show the same fastidiousness in all they do, whether in planning meals or cleaning the house.

ISFJs can often become pushovers due to their kindheartedness. They won't really seek recognition for their good works and cunning people around them can easily take credit for all their efforts. Nevertheless, their good work and virtuous attitude are valued and appreciated by those that know them. People that belong to this personality type will often need to be more assertive in order to let the world know of their noble actions. The ISFJs need to feel appreciated in order to boost their confidence and to stay happy.

Having an ISFJ for a workmate, friend, or family can be very rewarding. They give the most suitable advice and gifts! This is due to their sensitivity to other people's needs coupled with big-heartedness. Their words of advice are wise and earnest and the gifts they give are always from the heart. The ISFJs are dependable folks. They pull their weight and they make certain what needs to be done is done. And although they are introverted, they are able to make real friends and have relationships that are truly meaningful.

The ISFJs are contented to be backstage and they never really crave for the spotlight. Nevertheless, they don't want their hard work to go to waste or to go unnoticed. Individuals that belong to the ISFJ personality derive fulfillment when they are able to do quality work and produce results that can benefit the majority.

Chapter 2: The Strengths and Weaknesses of an ISFJ

ISFJ Strengths

Helpful

This group of individuals is always ready to reach out, offer advice, and lend a helping hand. They are willing to share knowledge and even resources when they think that these can benefit those around them.

Empathetic

People with this personality type are empathetic. They feel the pain and they share the joy of those they have just met and those they have strong connections with. They are sensitive folks that want to relieve others of any burden they are experiencing, if they have the power to do it.

Responsible

Any duties assigned to the ISFJ will surely get done and will be done well. ISFJ individuals are reliable workers, friends, and family members. They care for others and they understand the importance of honoring the responsibilities given to them.

Perfectionists

There is no place for substandard work, as far as the ISFJ is concerned. This person takes his tasks very seriously and he will guarantee only the best outcomes. He will often work on his duties painstakingly just to make sure that every detail is covered and that nothing negative reflects back on him. The ISFJs are a hardworking bunch.

Practical

The ISFJs are grounded people. This goes hand in hand with their sense of responsibility. They know what needs to be done at the moment and they are willing to work hard to make things happen.

Optimistic

You won't ever need to give an ISFJ a pep talk. In fact, they are the best people to motivate others with their enthusiasm and positive outlook on life. Anyone who meets an ISFJ will surely notice his high spirits.

Loyal

They make loyal employees, friends, and lovers. People that belong to this personality type are able to make strong connections with those they associate with. As a result, they have long-term friends and romantic relationships. Plus, they may work in a single company for a long time.

Achievers

Though, they may procrastinate, they eventually get things done. No projects are left hanging and no tasks or goals are disregarded or forgotten. These people will accomplish whatever needs to be accomplished, maybe just not right away, but all in good time.

ISFJ Weaknesses

Shy

These folks are not likely to start a conversation first and they won't be opening up to those they've just met. Other people will often misinterpret their shyness for snobbishness or even arrogance. It will take a long time to connect with an ISFJ, but when you do, they make the best of friends.

Humble

The modesty of the ISFJ can often be taken as lack of assertiveness. They don't announce their accomplishments and they rarely volunteer any information concerning their good deeds. As a result, many people don't know about their work and achievements. Also, some people may take credit for their hard work because they don't publicly announce that they were the ones behind the feat.

Don't Separate Personal and Professional Lives

The ISFJs want to be perfect in all parts of their lives. Their professional and personal lives are often closely related. They always want both to reflect positively on them. They think that a work problem could reflect on their personal lives and relationship troubles could reflect on their careers.

Don't Express Their Feelings

The ISFJ sibling, friend, colleague, or lover often won't say how he really feels about certain issues. They repress their feelings or don't show their emotions because they are very private people. They keep their reaction to themselves and are never vocal about it. As a result, the ISFJs can become stressed, and their inability to express their emotions freely could affect their mental and emotional health.

Stick to Tried and Tested Ways

People that belong to this group are perfectionists and they often stick to methods that have already been tried and tested. They do this because they want to minimize any errors. Consequently, they value traditions and are often reluctant to try new things.

Self-Sacrificing

Many ISFJs often carry too much workload. In their desire to help others, they burden themselves with tasks and problems that should be addressed by other individuals.

Chapter 3: The ISFJ as a Friend, Romantic Partner, and Parent

Friendships

A lot of individuals that have met an ISFJ would think of him as a dear friend. However, the ISFJ considers very few people his true friends. So even when you consider an ISFJ as your friend, he may not return the favor. The reason why many people regard the ISFJ individuals as friends is because of their enjoyable company and although, the ISFJs are kind people, they tend to be protective of themselves. They are very shy and wary about trusting other people with their friendship. Nevertheless, when they make a deep connection with someone, they become committed to the friendship. Therefore, in order for a person to be considered an ISFJ's friend, he will need to be in contact with him for a long time and consistently. For the ISFJs, friendship is not made in just one or two meetings. The connection will need to be established over time through consistent contact and quality communication. Trust will need to be built and the ISFJ will need to feel secure first before accepting the friendship of another.

ISFJs are valued friends because they are generous and self-sacrificing. They always give their full support to people they care about, whether it's in terms of financial, emotional, physical or spiritual assistance. The ISFJ friend is warm and he is always ready to uplift a friend. In return, he needs to feel supported by the people that he considers his friends. He needs to feel appreciated by his friends and he thrives on positive feedback. ISFJ individuals are able to create long-lasting friendships with those that can reciprocate the efforts they give as a friend. In case a friend takes the ISFJ's efforts for granted, the ISFJ will not hesitate to end the relationship. For sure, the ISFJ group makes the most loyal of friends. They stick by those they have faith in and they never betray another person's trust.

It is common for ISFJs to sacrifice their own happiness in order to make their friends feel happy. They can put their needs aside so that they can offer support to those that belong in their circle of friends. Consequently, the ISFJ may not be able to deal with his own urgent problems. It's up to the real friends of the ISFJ to remember how self-sacrificing this individual can be and to offer their support for him in return.

Romance

Meeting an ISFJ for a friend is not easy and it's more challenging to make a romantic connection with them due to their shyness. They are introverts and it's never easy for them to socialize with new people. So starting a romantic relationship with an ISFJ may not happen just like in the movies. A person who is interested in dating an ISFJ will need to invest a lot of time and effort in order to catch his attention and to make a connection. When it comes to romance, individuals that belong to the ISFJ group are looking for long-term relationships. Because their shyness makes meeting people hard for them, they will want to keep the relationships that they already have. But that is not the only reason. ISFJs are traditional people and they value the family and the home. For them, to love someone is not a game. They will take dating very seriously because they regard this as a crucial step for marriage and for building a family.

Those that have been in a relationship with the ISFJs can vouch for their kindness and generosity to their partners. They are sensitive and caring to those they love. Since the ISFJs are selfless, they will always put their partner's needs first, before their own. This trait makes them good lovers. Partners of the ISFJ need to encourage their lover to express his emotions and feelings more freely in their relationship. The ISFJ has a tendency to suppress his emotions in an effort to avoid conflict and to please his partner. Nevertheless, the ISFJ lover will need to learn to be more vocal and more expressive of his own needs in order to be happy in the relationship. His partner should help him to do this. If the ISFJ continues to suppress his feelings, he may end up having an outburst that could cause irreparable damage to the relationship. This is why ISFJ partners need to encourage their lovers to speak up more often and to say what's on their heart and mind, especially when it comes to issues that really matter to them.

Whether inside or outside the bedroom, the ISFJ lover longs for nothing but to give happiness to his partner. He will exert effort to make sure that his lover is satisfied in the relationship. The best romantic partners for the ISFJ are those that share the same ideals when it comes to love and family.

Parenthood

Children born to ISFJ parents are lucky to have doting parents. Most ISFJ parents are loving parents and they truly find happiness in caring for their young. Since the ISFJ are responsible individuals, their children will never worry about their needs. ISFJs are good providers to the family. They are hardworking folks that value their family. Hence, they will do all that they can to give their wives, husbands, and children all that they deserve in life.

Having ISFJ parents is very beneficial to impressionable minds. The ISFJs are kind, generous, and sympathetic people. They always try to do what is right in every situation. Young kids as well as adult children with ISFJ parents will always have good role models in their lives. The role of parents is very important to the ISFJs and they will take this duty very seriously. They will help their children to attain their goals and to have lives that are meaningful and worth living.

Chapter 4: Choosing the Best Career for an ISFJ

The ISFJ people are sensitive to their client's needs. Plus, they are meticulous workers. They pay attention to detail and they want the results to be perfect. In essence, that makes them good employees in any field. Nevertheless, these traits would make them excellent assistants. They are great at remembering important events such as anniversaries, birthdays, and other special occasions that would otherwise be forgotten in a busy workplace. They become valuable assistants to their bosses because of their keen eye for detail. They never miss anything important and they always make sure that every task is accomplished.

Due to the altruistic quality of ISFJs, they are the best advisers. They have a kind heart and they always want what's best for everybody. So, if they become counselors to people in authority such as the heads of a company or leaders of an organization, a large number of people will benefit. ISFJs have good hearts and although, they are too shy to become leaders themselves, they can share their good plans and intentions by counseling those that have the power to act.

ISFJs can thrive in careers that involve careful planning and organization. Being perfectionists who are very sensitive to details, they can become great engineers, architects, and IT staff. They enjoy creating plans and thinking things through. Their eye for detail is uncanny, and they love putting small parts together.

Since ISFJs are selfless, compassionate, and generous, they do well in medical careers. They can find happiness and fulfillment in assisting sick people, curing them, and making them feel more comfortable in their time of illness. Because they are sensitive, they can feel another person's pain and they are able to provide care and relief for their patients.

It's not uncommon to find the ISFJ among the teachers. Due to their innate desire to help others, the ISFJ will also find their life's meaning in imparting knowledge. Many ISFJs are in the academic profession because they want to share what they know to others. They also have a desire to help people improve their status in life and they do this by encouraging people to never stop learning.

The shyness of ISFJs can sometimes be a hindrance in the progress of their career. They might not want to be promoted to higher positions such as managerial positions for fear that they would always be in the spotlight. ISFJs work best when they are in the background. All they want is for their good performance to be recognized. They don't aim for high positions or high salaries. They are satisfied that they are able to do a good job, and their job satisfaction comes from being able to contribute to society.

People that belong to this personality type also work well in Human Resources because they have the ability to solve conflicts. If ever there are problems between employees, the ISFJ will be able to guide them into having a more peaceful and a more professional working relationship. ISFJs hate any form of conflict and they can help their colleagues get along and move in the same direction.

In a nutshell, ISFJs are happy in entry-level jobs and middle management positions. Them being introverted keeps them from advancing up the corporate ladder and claiming higher positions. Not that they want that, anyway. They are just happy to have good working conditions that allow them to find fulfillment.

Chapter 5: The ISFJ's Workplace Behavior and Ethics

Any kind of company can greatly flourish with ISFJs in their workforce. These employees are sincere, responsible, and hardworking—qualities that can help a company develop and progress. ISFJs make good colleagues, too. They help their coworkers, they are supportive, and they always want others to attain success. They are never competitive, spiteful, or malevolent—common traits that ambitious people show in the workplace in order to get ahead of others.

It is sure that ISFJs are dedicated workers. They are focused on giving a good performance at work and they inspire their colleagues to do the same. It is not uncommon for the ISFJ to help a colleague who might be struggling with his tasks at work. He is always willing to give advice, share his knowledge, or do additional work for a colleague.

If there are people in the workplace that are prone to causing conflicts, there are also those that do nothing to resolve it. However, ISFJs are the ones that either prevent or solve the conflict. Individuals that have the ISFJ personality feel uneasy when there are people around them that don't get along. He will find ways to make the conflicting parties find common ground. Since these people are very sensitive, they are able to perceive the feelings of those around them and they can help solve issues that could otherwise affect their work.

The ISFJ Subordinate

ISFJs are excellent followers. They understand the hierarchy and the responsibilities that go with every position in the company. Therefore, it's not difficult for the ISFJ to respect his superiors. He understands that these people have worked hard to attain their positions and those that work hard deserve to be rewarded. In general, ISFJs are not ambitious so they are not coveting the jobs of their bosses. It is enough for the ISFJ to be praised and recognized for his good work. However, that sometimes fails to happen because ISFJs are humble folks. They never brag or announce their achievements. As a result, their efforts often go unnoticed, and this can make ISFJs very frustrated. In order to keep the ISFJ subordinate inspired and enthusiastic, his boss should recognize all his hard work. Once the ISFJ feels appreciated, he will continue to offer good service to the people and the company he works for.

Having ISFJ workers means having loyal employees. They are able to provide long-term quality service to companies that, they think, deserve their loyalty. While it may sound as though ISFJs are the perfect employees, they also have some weaknesses at work. They are resistant to change and may not receive new principles very well. Bosses of ISFJs need to present their case carefully to the ISFJ in order for him to accept the changes and to remain loyal to the company.

The ISFJ Colleague

Although the ISFJ is shy, he gets along with his colleagues very well. He is cooperative and is regarded as a team player. He can work with almost every type of personality due to his big heart. Once his coworkers get to know him well, they find a warm person inside his shell. It can be difficult to get close to the ISFJ colleague at first—and some might make the mistake of thinking that he is snooty—but constant contact with him in the workplace will reveal that the ISFJ colleague is a nice person.

The ISFJ Boss

Many ISFJs don't really aim for managerial positions because of their introverted attitude. They don't want to be in the spotlight and would actually be more comfortable in lower job positions. Nevertheless, ISFJs are hard workers so naturally they will be promoted and will claim higher positions in life. As managers, ISFJs are still good workers. And if they are dedicated and loyal subordinates, they will make exemplary bosses.

The trouble with the ISFJ in the managerial position is his inability to assume an authoritarian role. Individuals that possess this type of personality are shy, kind, and they have an aversion to conflict. It can be a difficult task for him to give orders to his subordinates and to be strict in implementing rules. ISFJ bosses may not be able to handle a situation where his subordinates disagree with him and refuse to follow his orders. And although he can effectively deal with conflicts as a colleague, his role as a superior prevents him from achieving the same goal. As a boss, he will need to make his subordinates follow his orders. It's one of the challenges that the ISFJ in the managerial position has to face.

In general, the ISFJ is well respected by his subordinates. He is a hardworking person that inspires his subordinates to excel in their jobs. Those that work under him see his kindness, generosity, and dedication to his work. In addition, the ISFJ boss is an achiever and, as we've said more than once before, a perfectionist. He makes a capable leader to all those under his wing. These are traits that make a boss truly respectable and worth following.

The ISFJ boss will have no trouble creating harmonious relationships with his subordinates. Even with his shy demeanor, his kindheartedness makes him approachable as a boss. His subordinates will never feel intimidated to approach him about possible work concerns as well as to ask for personal help. However, the ISFJ boss needs to be on his toes as some subordinates can take advantage of his generosity. For instance, lazy employees can appeal to his kindness and may try to avoid doing the tasks assigned to them. Also, the ISFJ manager can at times be too understanding instead of meting out rightful punishments to erring employees.

When it comes to his managerial duties, the ISFJ boss is efficient. These individuals have usually reached their managerial position by promotion and through hard work so they understand their duties very well. The ISFJ make competent leaders when they have to be in-charge. Again, due to them being perfectionists, it could put pressure on the subordinates to always do their best. In a way, that is a good thing, and ISFJs are excellent at overseeing the work of their subordinates. On the flip side, this could lead to a subordinate becoming too anxious over the fact that the boss is a perfectionist, and suffer from stress as a result.

Conclusion

One thing that anyone can say about ISFJs is that they are dedicated and reliable people. They have good heads on top of their shoulders and many can appreciate their practicality. ISFJs make loyal, trustworthy friends that one can keep for a whole lifetime. They are excellent parents, siblings, and colleagues because of their generosity and kindness. And any woman or man will be lucky to have an ISFJ as a romantic partner.

People that belong to the ISFJ personality type can enrich the lives of those around them. Through their altruistic characteristics, people remember that not all individuals are selfish, greedy, and spiteful. The ISFJ folks give hope to us all that there are still good people out there, although this group comprises only 13% of the world's population.

Knowing about the distinct traits of the ISFJ group can help us better understand and appreciate those that have this personality. Like all other personality types, ISFJs have strengths and weaknesses. Having read this book, you now have an idea about what these are. Hopefully, you can help your ISFJ brother, sister, friend, wife, or husband to overcome the weaknesses of the ISFJ personality trait. And if you know an ISFJ who has not yet discovered his strengths, then perhaps you can lead him, so that he can achieve happiness and fulfillment. By understanding the personality traits of the ISFJ, you can also help yourself (if you happen to be an ISFJ) find your perfect career and your perfect partner in life.

Finally, I'd like to thank you for purchasing this book! If you enjoyed it or found it helpful, I'd greatly appreciate it if you'd take a moment to leave a review on Amazon. Thank you!

Printed in Great Britain
by Amazon